AF421966

THIS BOOK BELONGS TO:

____

FOR ALL THE SWEET KIDS WITH BIG IMAGINATIONS—MAY YOU ALWAYS FIND FRIENDS AS DELIGHTFUL AS A CUPCAKE (JUST TRY NOT TO EAT THEM!).

HI!

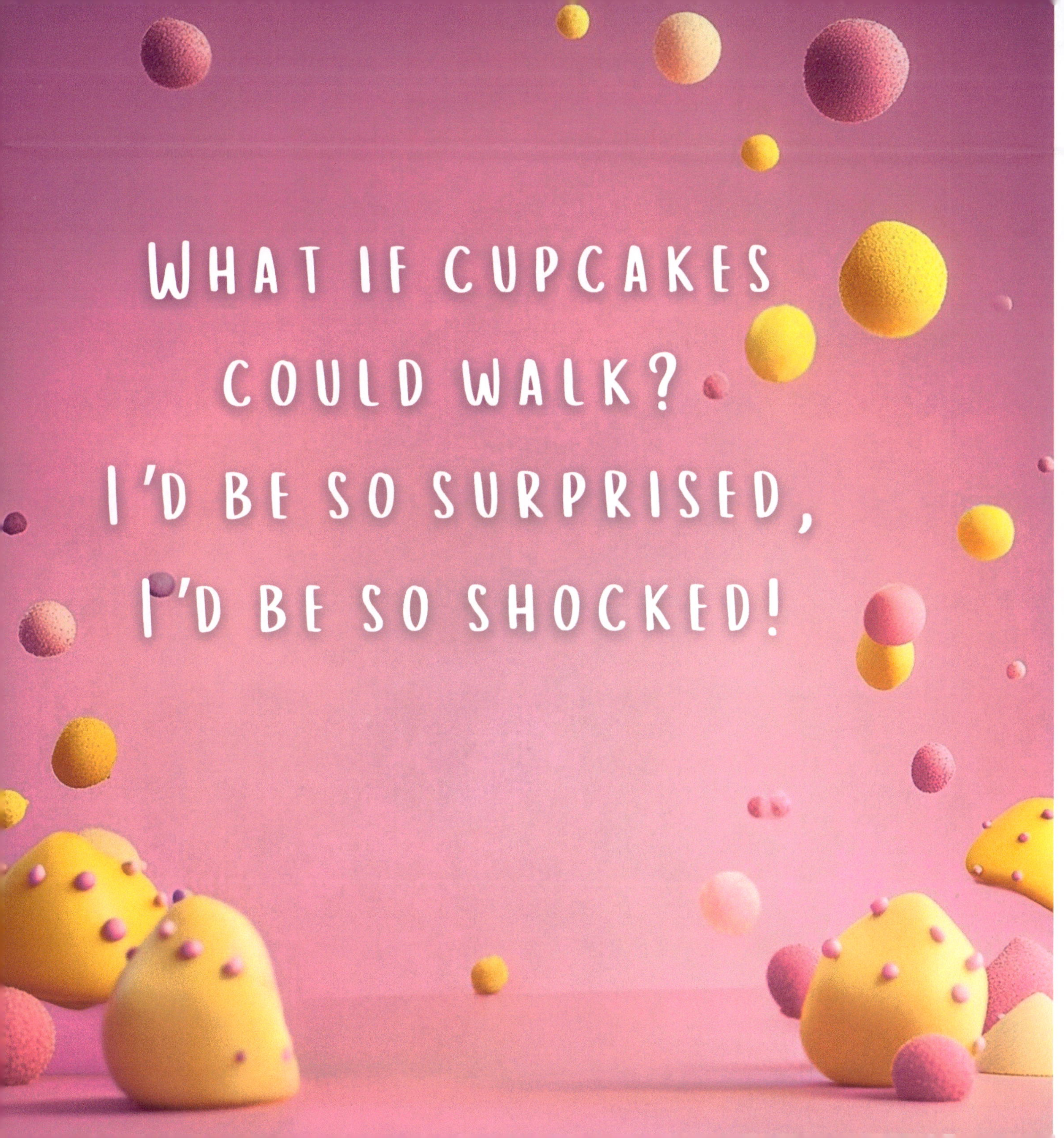

What if cupcakes could walk?
I'd be so surprised,
I'd be so shocked!

Imagine it wiggled
right up to say,
"Hey!"
Wouldn't that make
for the silliest day?

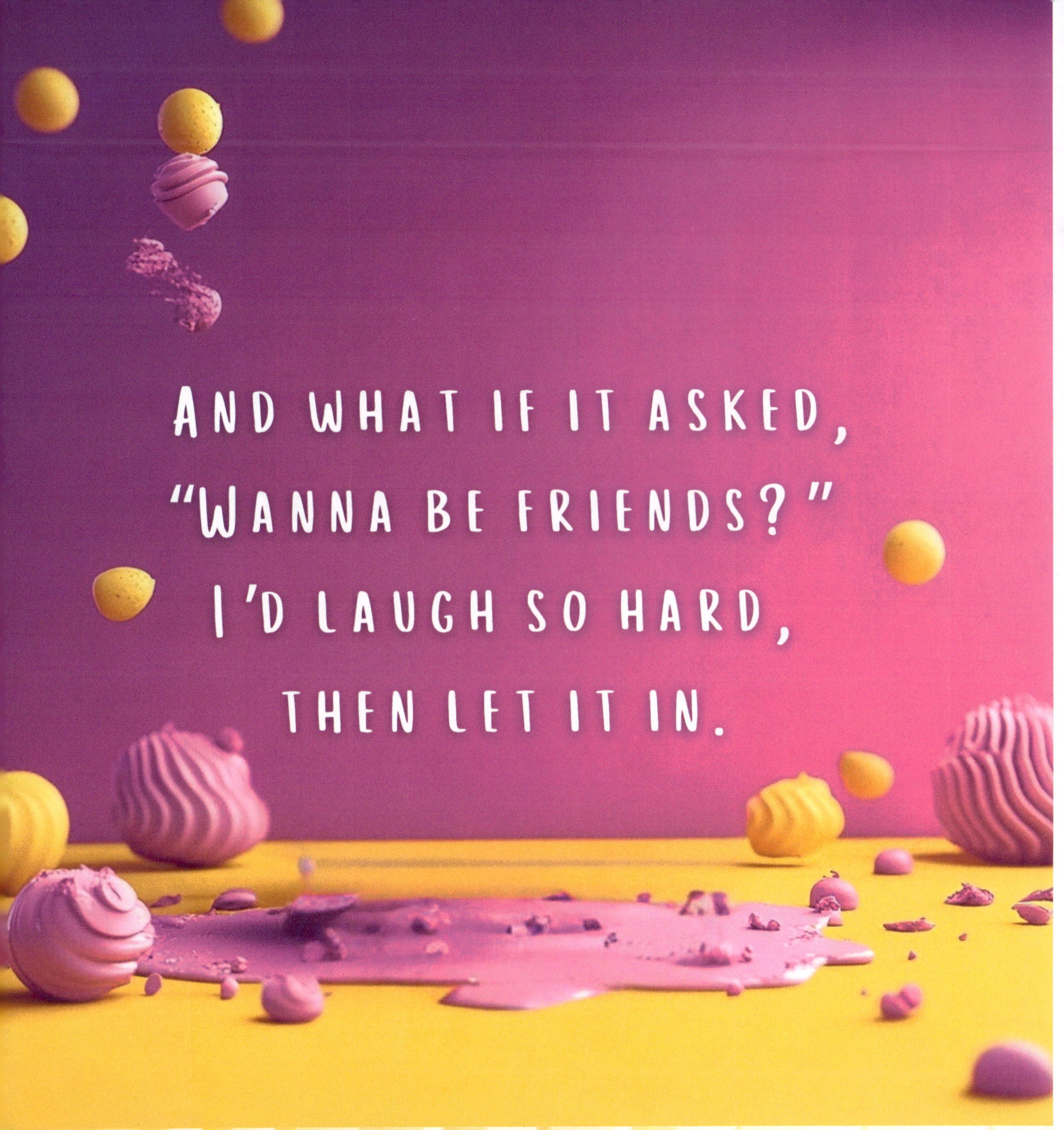
And what if it asked,
"Wanna be friends?"
I'd laugh so hard,
then let it in.

But wait a second. Let's think this through, Cupcakes aren't friends like me and you!

SURE, THEY'RE SWEET
BUT THEY SMELL SO YUMMY,
I MIGHT NEED A TREAT TO
FILL MY TUMMY

If I take one bite
—oh dear, oh no!
Now my cupcake friend
is crumbs, uh-oh!

No more chatting,
no more fun,
My cupcake friendship,
that's all done.

Remember...
We're talking about cupcakes here!

Imagine being friends with one—

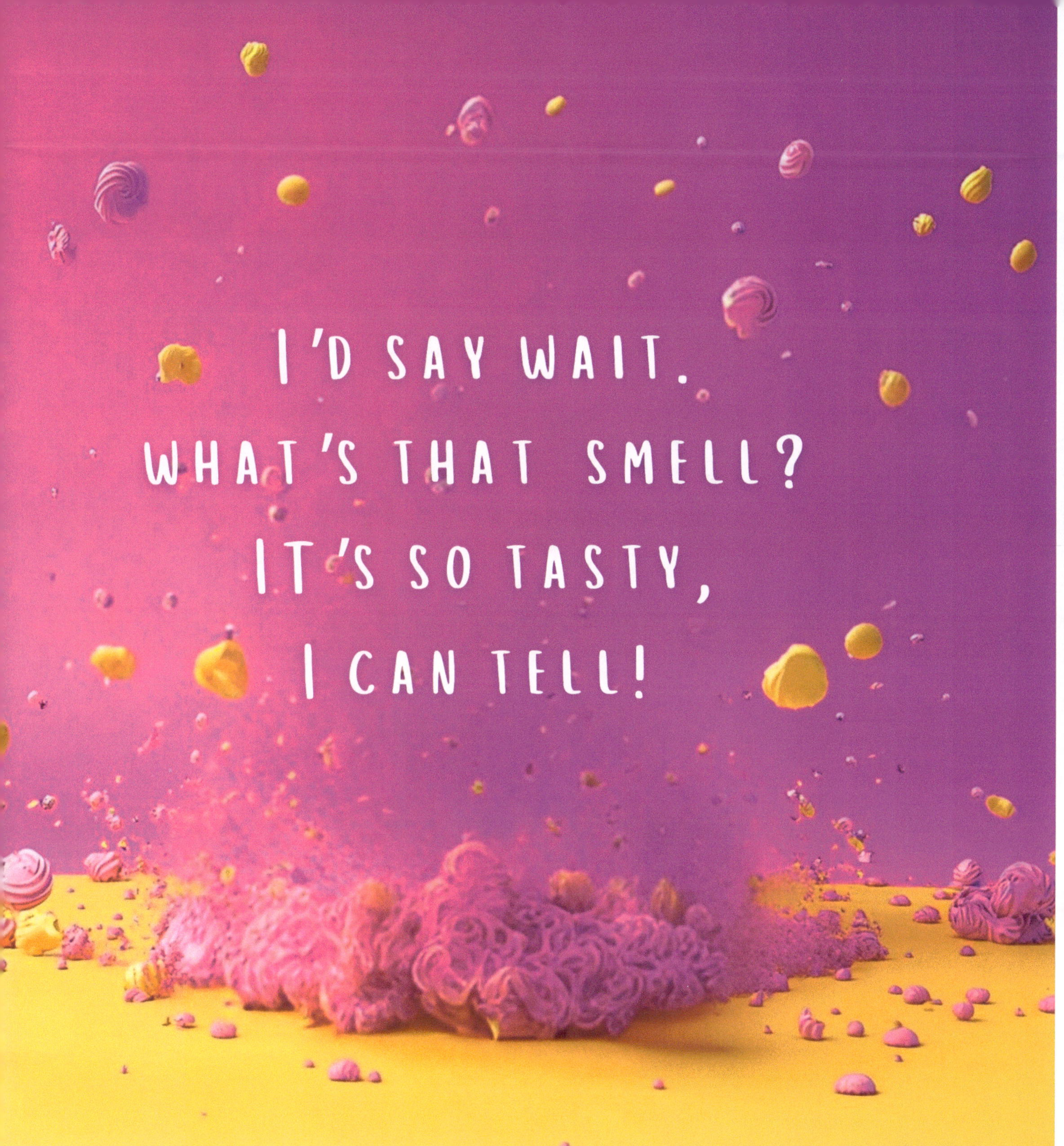

I'D SAY WAIT.
WHAT'S THAT SMELL?
IT'S SO TASTY,
I CAN TELL!

A tiny nibble
And oops!
That was your friend,
you silly goose.

Now look around.
Do you see any cupcakes?

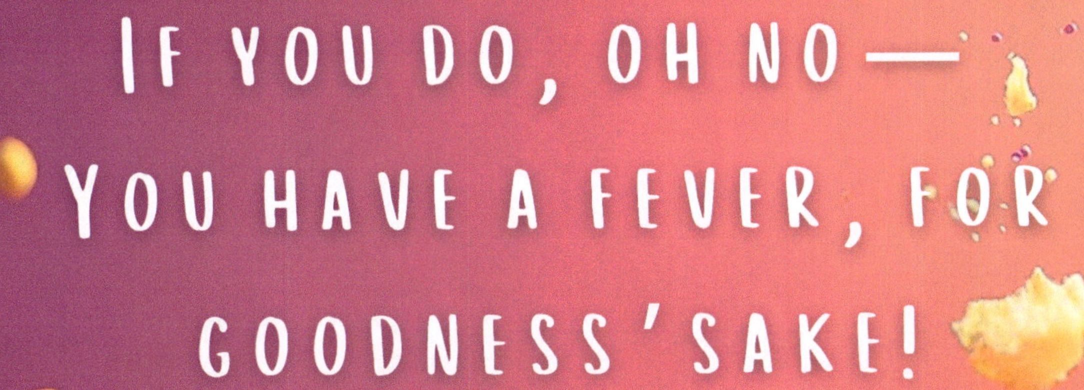
If you do, oh no—
you have a fever, for
goodness' sake!

Because you should be
seeing people,
not frosting or
sprinkles!

Cupcakes aren't for being friends,
But for yummy tummy tickles.